# ALL IN

The New York Giants Official 2011 Season & Super Bowl XLVI Commemorative

SKYBOX PRESS, SAN DIEGO  •  ABRAMS, NEW YORK

This pregame ritual symbolizes what would become a battle cry for the 2011 Giants and their fans: *All In.*

Eli Manning calls the snap count during a Week 10 road game at San Francisco.

# CONTENTS

New York celebrates its Super Bowl champions with a ticker-tape parade through the Canyon of Heroes on February 7, 2012.

## BY TOM COUGHLIN

The night before Super Bowl XLVI, as our team convened for the final time before competing in the greatest game of our lives, I told our players that I love them. I spoke of the late John Wooden and his Pyramid of Success. "At the very top of the pyramid is the phrase Competitive Toughness," I explained; however, later in his life Coach Wooden revised that, saying that Competitive Toughness should be replaced with Love. "I speak for all of the coaches when I say that you guys have taught us what love really is," I said. "And I am man enough to tell you guys that I love you."

I let the players know how much I wanted this moment for them. "The ring is everything," I said. "There is no sense in playing if you can't ever get the feeling of standing on top of the mountain and saying, 'I am the king of the hill.'"

The theme we talked about over and over developed the first day we gathered in preseason: Finish. Finish the play, finish the game, finish the season. "Teamwork is the essence of life; it is not about the individual, it is about the team. Championships are won by teams who love one another, who enjoy and respect one another, who play for and support one another. No matter what happens, no matter what they throw at us, no matter what comes about, we will fight from play to play, and we will persevere until victory is ours."

In the Super Bowl, there is always an X-factor. "Who will step up and be the guy that makes the play that makes the difference?" I asked. "Big players make big plays in big games—and it doesn't get any bigger than this."

"Fight," I urged. "Fight as you have never fought before. When a warrior fights not for himself but for his brothers, his most happily sought goal is neither glory nor fame, but rather to defend what he believes in."

I believe that what matters most is not how we reach the finish line, but rather who crosses the finish line with us. "There are millions of people out there that you have inspired, people who may be down on their luck or have been dealt a bad blow who, now, because of this team, believe that anything is possible.

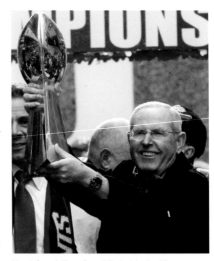

Head Coach Tom Coughlin holds the Vince Lombardi Trophy aloft during the Giants Super Bowl victory celebration.

"When the gun goes off at the end of the Super Bowl and we have won the game," I said, "you will turn to a teammate or a coach and you will grab him because you want to share the moment. Then you will look up into the stands, and you'll see your wife, your mother and father, your children, and you'll want to share the moment with them because they are also World Champions."

That night we showed the team highlights from the postseason set to the Phil Collins song "In the Air Tonight." *I've been waiting for this moment all my life.* What an incredible phrase to leave us with.

"Let's go climb this next mountain together," I said. "Let's be World Champions."

# Introduction

## BY JOHN MARA & STEVE TISCH

Thank you to all of our players, our coaches, our staff and our fans on behalf the Mara and Tisch families for making us World Champions for the second time in five years. I want you to know how much this means to my family. This is not just a business to us—it's personal. We've been here with this team since the beginning, in 1925, and what you will see in this book is a capsule of a team that embodied everything we've aspired to over those years. We are the World Champions once again, and to have an organization that is universally respected and, to my thinking, second to none, is very special indeed. So thank you Jerry Reese, Tom Coughlin and all the players, coaches and staff and fans for making this dream of ours a reality.

—*John Mara*

It is very difficult to preach teamwork if the two people in charge of the team don't practice it. Tom Coughlin and Jerry Reese are both committed to selflessness and a team-first approach and an undying responsibility to their players and this amazing organization. Part of the winning foundation is resiliency as well as toughness. The men who made up the 2011 New York Giants exemplify what Coach Coughlin preaches. They are resilient. They are the most resilient. They rebounded when they were 7-7 to win the Super Bowl. And they are tough, as they proved once again by going on the road to Green Bay, then to San Francisco and then to Indianapolis to defeat a great New England Patriots team. They finished the 2011 season in the grandest form possible, by adding the New York Giants' fourth Lombardi Trophy to our display case.

—*Steve Tisch*

New York Giants co-owners John Mara, *left*, and Steve Tisch enjoy the Super Bowl XLVI championship ceremony at City Hall.

The Giants set aside their numerous injuries, their six-game losing streak against the Eagles and the hype that had made their opponents so popular to the football public to earn a rewarding 29-16 road victory in Philadelphia.

The Giants offense set the pace. Quarterback Eli Manning completed 16 of 23 passes for 254 yards, four touchdowns and no interceptions, and his 145.7 passer rating was his highest ever in a full game. Wide receiver Victor Cruz stepped in for the inactive Mario Manningham and scored his first two NFL touchdowns on receptions of 74 and 28 yards and had three catches for 110 yards. Running back Ahmad Bradshaw had team-high totals of 86 rushing yards and five catches, including the 18-yard touchdown pass that clinched the victory and sent the fans scurrying from their seats. Running back Brandon Jacobs also had a 40-yard touchdown catch.

The defense controlled the Eagles offense. Cornerback Aaron Ross intercepted two passes and safety Kenny Phillips had a third pick. Phillips, defensive end Jason Pierre-Paul and rookie linebacker Jacquian Williams had nine tackles apiece (all of Williams' stops were solo). Pierre-Paul had two sacks. Linebacker Michael Boley made a huge tackle to stop an Eagles bid on fourth down. Safety Deon Grant, who played most of the game in place of middle linebacker Greg Jones, had seven tackles (six solo).

The game was like a three-act play. Act I belonged to the Giants, who shut out the Eagles 14-0 in the first quarter. Philadelphia controlled Act II, outscoring the Giants 16-0 in the second and third quarters. Running back LeSean McCoy ran for Philly's only touchdown, and rookie Alex Henery kicked three field goals. But Big Blue stormed back in Act III, blanking the Eagles 15-0 in the fourth and winning a game—for the first time in nearly a year—when trailing after three quarters.

"It's always great to beat the Eagles on their home field, because they have great players. We felt coming in that we could beat these guys because we should have last year. We knew we had to win the fourth quarter. This year, unlike last year, we won the last eight minutes of the game. It was a big win for us." —Eli Manning

*Above*: Jason Pierre-Paul goes for the sack on Eagles QB Michael Vick during a 29-16 Week 3 road win.
*Opposite*: Ahmad Bradshaw leaps in front of Philadelphia's Nnamdi Asomugha for a second-half touchdown.

Antrel Rolle rallies his teammates on the sidelines.

*Clockwise from top left*: Eli Manning points out the defense; Jacquian Williams wraps up Eagles RB LeSean McCoy; Team captains Justin Tuck and Manning get instructions from Coach Coughlin before the coin toss; Mathias Kiwanuka pursues the ball.

*Above left*: David Diehl congratulates Ahmad Bradshaw after a second-half touchdown. *Above right*: Victor Cruz stretches over the goal line despite the efforts of the Eagles Jarrad Page and Nnamdi Asomugha.

Aaron Ross leaps over Philadelphia's DeSean Jackson for a second-half interception of Eagles QB Mike Kafka.

# TRUE GIANTS
## VICTOR CRUZ
Wide Receiver

It's a struggle to remember when you didn't know the name Victor Cruz or his salsa dance, but there was indeed a time not too long ago. Undrafted in 2010, Cruz flashed his brilliance in a preseason game as a rookie but was put on the backburner with a season-ending injury. Then 2011 rolled around, and with a lackluster camp and a few early drops, Cruz still wasn't what he is today. That all changed in Week 3. His life and your life as a fan would never be the same after he torched the Eagles on their home turf for a first-quarter 74-yard touchdown, the first of his emerging career. He added another 28-yarder in the victory over the bitter rivals at the other end of the New Jersey Turnpike; that's when the dancing began—and it continued even after he and his teammates reached the steps of City Hall at the Super Bowl XLVI parade. His 1,536 receiving yards in a single season broke Amani Toomer's former team record, set in 2002. Ninety-nine of those yards came on one play that was widely regarded as the turning point of the season. Playing what was essentially a playoff game with a postseason berth on the line, the Giants found themselves facing a 7-3 deficit nearing halftime of their Week 16 bout with the Jets. On third-and-10 from the Giants 1-yard line, Cruz was looking to avoid the fourth three-and-out of the half. He got a whole lot more. After catching Eli Manning's short pass, Cruz faked his way past several defenders and sprinted down the Jets sideline for a 99-yard go-ahead touchdown. Cruz finished the game with 164 yards on three catches. He followed up the next week with 178 yards to help clinch the NFC East title against the Cowboys. The big stage of the postseason wouldn't slow him down as he hauled in 10 catches for 157 yards against the stingy San Francisco defense in the NFC Championship and scored the first touchdown of Super Bowl XLVI.

In a game with an eerily similar conclusion to the finishes of Super Bowls XLII and XLVI, Eli Manning threw two touchdown passes in the final 3:03, including the 1-yard game-winning pass to tight end Jake Ballard with just 15 seconds left. The Giants defeated the Patriots, 24-20, three months before the teams would meet again in the Super Bowl.

The teams traded the lead three times in the fourth quarter—just as they did in their first Super Bowl clash. In that game, the Giants ruined New England's perfect season; this time, they ended the Patriots' 20-game regular season home winning streak.

Manning completed 20 of 39 passes for 250 yards—179 in the decisive second half. Neither team scored a point in the first half, and the third quarter ended with the Giants holding a 10-3 lead. The Patriots took their first lead at 13-10 with 7:08 remaining. Manning led the Giants on an 8-play, 85-yard drive aided by a 35-yard pass interference penalty on Patriots cornerback Kyle Arrington. It ended when Manning floated a perfect 10-yard touchdown pass to Mario Manningham on third-and-five for a 17-13 lead, a precursor to the thrilling finish.

New England took a three-point lead on quarterback Tom Brady's 14-yard touchdown pass to tight end Ron Gronkowski with 1:36 remaining. Manning and the Giants responded with an 80-yard drive highlighted by Ballard's clutch 28-yard reception on third-and-10. Four plays and a pass interference penalty later, Manning found Ballard for the winning touchdown.

We had plenty of time to go down there and get the touchdown. You never want to take it into overtime. When we needed touchdowns, when we had to step up, guys continued to make plays at the right time. It's a great quality. When we need it, guys are making big plays. —Eli Manning

*Clockwise from top left:* Patriots QB Tom Brady congratulates Eli Manning after the Giants' 24-20 Week 9 road win; Ramses Barden eyes the end zone; Tom Coughlin is a study in intensity; D.J. Ware celebrates in the fourth quarter. *Opposite:* David Diehl swarms Manning after a 10-yard touchdown pass to Mario Manningham with 3:03 remaining.

*Above left*: Justin Tuck and the defense pressured Tom Brady into two sacks and two interceptions. *Above right*: Jake Ballard makes an acrobatic catch in front of the Patriots Tracy White during a fourth-quarter drive.

Mario Manningham gathers in a touchdown pass next to New England's Kyle Arrington to regain the lead at 17-13.

Mathias Kiwanuka flies at Tom Brady during the fourth quarter.

*Above left*: Victor Cruz works for extra yards before being tackled by the Patriots Devin McCourty. *Above right*: Eli Manning rolls outside the pocket looking to complete one of his 39 pass attempts.

# TRUE GIANTS

## KEVIN BOOTHE
Offensive Line

Championships are won at the line of scrimmage. For the Giants, that means versatility, and no one embodied that better than Kevin Boothe on the offensive line. Already in a transition period with the departure of two key veterans, the O-line suffered several injuries and ailments, creating more gaps throughout the season. Boothe, the Ivy Leaguer from Cornell, plugged those holes and started at three different positions in 2011: center and both guard positions. He would go on to do much more than spot duty as he became the starting left guard for the season's final six games. Boothe played in all 20 games and started 13 of them, including the final 10 through the Super Bowl. On both sides of the ball, the Giants battled injuries from the very beginning, but their opponents weren't about to show sympathy. The way Big Blue responded and relied on their depth at all positions was a major thread in 2011's storyline. And while every team has its share of superstars, the Giants were the only one with a Boothe to count on in 2011.

# 3 at DALLAS

December 11, 2011 · Cowboys Stadium · Giants 37 – Cowboys 34

For the sixth time in the 2011 season—a franchise record—Eli Manning led the Giants to victory in a game where the Giants trailed or were tied in the fourth quarter. Manning orchestrated this latest comeback in Cowboys Stadium with two touchdowns in the final 3:14 to defeat Dallas, 37-34, in a game that featured eight lead changes. The victory snapped a four-game losing streak.

The Giants trailed 34-22 after wide-open wide receiver Dez Bryant caught quarterback Tony Romo's fourth touchdown pass with 5:41 remaining in the fourth quarter. Manning led the Giants on an 8-play, 80-yard drive that ended with an 8-yard touchdown pass to Jake Ballard, which cut the deficit to 34-29. After Dallas went three-and-out, the Giants took possession at their own 42-yard line with 2:12 remaining.

The game-winning drive began with a 21-yard pass to Ballard. After the two-minute warning, Manning threw to Victor Cruz for 9 yards. Twice the Cowboys were penalized 5 yards, the second time for a hold by former Giant Frank Walker. That gave the Giants a first down at the Dallas 19-yard line with 1:21 left. Another throw to Ballard gained 18 yards then, two plays later, Brandon Jacobs scored the game-winner on a 1-yard run with 46 seconds left. It was Jacobs' 56th career rushing touchdown, breaking Tiki Barber's franchise record.

On the last two drives, Manning completed eight of 11 passes for 102 yards and a touchdown. The victory was preserved when defensive end Jason Pierre-Paul blocked kicker Dan Bailey's 47-yard field goal attempt as time expired.

"I can never remember a season like this, where almost every game is right down to the wire. I was happy because we needed to have a locker room celebration. We have been starving for that." —Tom Coughlin

*Above*: D.J. Ware fights for more yards in a 37-34 Week 14 road win against Dallas.
*Opposite*: Jason Pierre-Paul registers one of his two sacks of Cowboys QB Tony Romo.

*Above left*: Travis Beckum and the Cowboys Mike Jenkins fight for a pass. *Above right*: Deon Grant and Dave Tollefson stop Dallas RB DeMarco Murray, who fractured an ankle on the play.

Eli Manning lets fly one of his 47 pass attempts; he completed 27 for 400 yards and two touchdowns.

Deon Grant hauls down Cowboys RB Felix Jones as Aaron Ross converges on the play.

*Above left*: Jake Ballard contributed to the win with four catches in the game. *Above right*: Victor Cruz beats the Cowboys Orlando Scandrick.

# TRUE GIANTS
## JASON PIERRE-PAUL
Defensive End

While the defense sputtered at times, Jason Pierre-Paul's motor was going full speed the entire season. Giants faithful saw glimpses of his tenacity as a rookie in 2010, when he recorded 4.5 sacks, but he was still considered a raw talent. However, it was that unmolded ability and athleticism that made him so dynamic and allowed the coaching staff to teach him the Giants way. He absorbed it all while the team—and opponents—saw what he could become in 2011. Pierre-Paul, known colloquially as JPP, opened up with two sacks in the first game of his second NFL season and notched 7.5 in the first six games. He finished the regular season with 16.5 sacks and seven passes defended and became a true star during the Week 14 victory in Dallas. After having already forced a safety and a fumble, JPP showed just how relentless his game is and blocked what would have been a game-tying field goal to put the Giants ahead in the neck-and-neck race for the NFC East. "It just comes from the heart," he said after the game. "Ever since I was young, when I started playing football I didn't know too much, but I've had in my heart, just run." He was named the Defensive Player of the Week for his big game in Dallas and again for his Week 16 performance against the Jets (he was named NFC Defensive Player of the Month in December). During the Super Bowl week, defensive line coach Robert Nunn said he stays up at night just thinking about how high the ceiling is for JPP's legacy.

Talk never seemed so cheap and playing a game was never as sweet for the Giants as it was the day before Christmas in MetLife Stadium.

After a week listening to the Jets sling verbal barbs in their direction, the Giants arrived at the shared stadium to find their Super Bowl championship logos had been covered with a black curtain by the home team Jets. The Giants answered in the best possible fashion. They took the lead on a franchise-record 99-yard touchdown pass to wide receiver Victor Cruz in the second quarter and never relinquished it, delivering a 29-14 decision over the Jets.

The game, and the Giants season, turned on an event that hadn't previously occurred in the 87-year history of the franchise—a 99-yard play. On third-and-10 from the Giants own 1-yard line, Manning threw to the right side to Cruz, who caught the ball at the 11, eluded tackle attempts by cornerbacks Antonio Cromartie and Kyle Wilson then took off down the sideline. Safety Eric Smith lunged at Cruz near midfield, but the speedy receiver skipped away and sped to the end zone for a 10-7 lead with 2:12 remaining in the first half.

In addition to the Cruz's record-setting touchdown, the Giants scored on a pair of rushing touchdowns by Ahmad Bradshaw, two field goals by kicker Lawrence Tynes and a safety when defensive tackle Chris Canty sacked Jets quarterback Mark Sanchez in the end zone.

This game belonged to the Giants defense. The Jets ran 89 plays and held the ball for 36:06, 14 minutes longer than the Giants, but the Jets averaged only 3.7 yards per play and managed only 2 touchdowns in 16 offensive possessions.

> *We played great team defense. We were relentless. We forced some turnovers. We never buckled. We kept our eyes on the prize. We are in playoff mode right now. We understand that and our coaches did a great job of preparing us all week. We had a game plan and we stuck to it 100 percent.* —Antrel Rolle

*Above top*: Ahmad Bradshaw pounded out 54 rushing yards on 15 carries in a 29-14 Week 16 road win. *Above bottom*: Rookie LB Greg Jones stepped into the starting lineup after Jonathan Goff tore his ACL. *Opposite*: Jets WR Santonio Holmes gets nowhere against Corey Webster and Deon Grant.

Jacquian Williams bats down a second-quarter pass by Jets QB Mark Sanchez.

Deon Grant delivers a hit on the Jets Dustin Keller, one of Grant's five solo tackles.

*Clockwise from top left*: Kenny Phillips intercepts a pass in the fourth quarter; Victor Cruz had three catches for a whopping 164 yards; Brandon Jacobs celebrates with fans following the win; Justin Tuck strikes a pose after sacking Jets QB Mark Sanchez.

The offensive line gave Eli Manning the time and protection he needed.

# TRUE GIANTS
## AHMAD BRADSHAW
Running Back

While the Giants rushing attack struggled to find consistency all year, The Bulldog fought for every yard he gained in 2011. Ahmad Bradshaw was the primary back for the second straight season. Despite again battling foot issues, he rushed for 659 yards on 171 carries and nine touchdowns in 12 regular season games. Missing the entire month of November due to injury, Bradshaw returned at the tail end of the Giants' four-game losing streak. From then on, Bradshaw played through the pain as he helped the Giants win three of their last four to clinch the NFC East title. He scored four touchdowns in the final three weeks, including two against the Jets on Christmas Eve. When the Giants' running game came together in the postseason, Bradshaw averaged 4.3 yards per carry and famously scored the go-ahead 6-yard touchdown in Super Bowl XLVI, taking a seat in the end zone with 57 seconds remaining in the game.

With their season, the division title and their playoff aspirations down to a one-game, do-or-die situation, the Giants responded with an impressive and memorable victory, jumping out to a 21-point lead in the first half and going on to defeat Dallas, 31-14, in MetLife Stadium.

With their second straight victory, the Giants ended the season with a 9-7 record, one game better than the Cowboys, securing the NFC East Championship and earning their first division title and first postseason berth since 2008.

The Giants followed the same path that had brought them to so many victories—Eli Manning throwing passes and Victor Cruz catching them. Manning completed 24 of 33 passes for 346 yards, three touchdowns and no interceptions for a passer rating of 136.7. Cruz caught six of those balls for a career-high 178 yards and a 29.7-yard average.

Manning threw touchdown passes of 74 yards to Cruz, 10 yards to Ahmad Bradshaw and 4 yards to wide receiver Hakeem Nicks. Bradshaw also scored on a 5-yard run and Lawrence Tynes kicked a 28-yard field goal.

Dallas scored on two touchdown passes of 34 yards and 5 yards to wide receiver Laurent Robinson in the second half, but the Giants sacked Tony Romo six times, intercepted him once and stopped him on a quarterback sneak on a key fourth down early in the fourth quarter.

> " NFC East Champions—that is a great thing to hear. I won't get tired of hearing that over and over again. " —Tom Coughlin

*Above*: Ahmad Bradshaw celebrates after scoring on a 10-yard touchdown pass, his second touchdown of the game in a 31-14 Week 17 home win over Dallas. *Opposite*: Jason Pierre-Paul records a sack against Cowboys QB Tony Romo.

Eli Manning hands off to Brandon Jacobs during the first half.

*Above left*: Mathias Kiwanuka makes one of his five tackles against Dallas; he also recovered a fumble. *Above right*: Victor Cruz celebrates after catching one of his six receptions for 178 yards, including a touchdown.

*Clockwise from top left*: Henry Hynoski fights the Cowboys Sean Lee for extra yards; Devin Thomas returns a kick in the second half; Chris Canty pumps up his teammates; Eli Manning calls signals before taking the snap from David Baas.

Osi Umenyiora, *left*, and Justin Tuck celebrate after Tuck sacked Tony Romo.

# TRUE GIANTS
## ANTREL ROLLE
Safety

Losing on a last-second touchdown in Super Bowl XLIII when he played for the Arizona Cardinals always stayed with Antrel Rolle. He decided to join the Giants in 2010 in part to have an opportunity to contend for a title each season. While admitting he questioned whether it was the right fit during his first season, Rolle came to understand Tom Coughlin's approach through numerous talks with the head coach. Rolle then became a vocal leader in the locker room and challenged his teammates to give everything they had on the field during games and practices. It wasn't all lip service for the safety, who filled holes in all packages on the defense. In the box or back in coverage, Rolle played wherever defensive coordinator Perry Fewell needed him on any given week and led the team with 96 tackles in 2011. He recorded 24 tackles in four postseason games en route to getting back to the Super Bowl and exorcising those demons with a victory. Along the way, he became a formidable leader on the Giants defense.

# GIANT MOMENTS

## 2011: A Season of Milestones

**September 19, 2011 vs. St. Louis**

Michael Boley's 65-yard fumble return for a touchdown

Domenik Hixon's 22-yard touchdown from Eli Manning

**September 25, 2011 at Philadelphia**

Victor Cruz's 74-yard touchdown from Eli Manning

**October 2, 2011 at Arizona**

Osi Umenyiora's two sacks in his season debut

**December 4, 2011 vs. Green Bay**

Two touchdowns in the last 3:36

Travis Beckum's 67-yard touchdown from Eli Manning

**December 11, 2011 at Dallas**

Jason Pierre-Paul's safety and blocked field goal

Two touchdowns in the last 3:14

**January 15, 2012 at Green Bay**

Hakeem Nicks' 66-yard touchdown from Eli Manning

Chase Blackburn's 40-yard fumble return

Hakeem Nicks' 37-yard Hail Mary catch from Eli Manning

**January 22, 2012 at San Francisco**

Mario Manningham's 17-yard touchdown from Eli Manning

During the regular season, the Giants set franchise records with 6,161 total yards and 4,734 net passing yards. Eli Manning set Giants marks with 589 passes and 359 completions. Victor Cruz established a team record with 1,536 receiving yards while catching 82 passes, and Hakeem Nicks had 1,192 yards to give the Giants two 1,000-yard receivers for the first time in franchise history. On defense, second-year pro Jason Pierre-Paul had 16.5 sacks, the fourth-highest total in team history.

Two touchdowns
in the last 3:37

October 16, 2011
vs. Buffalo

Corey Webster's
two interceptions

Ahmad Bradshaw's
three touchdowns

November 6, 2011
at New England

Jake Ballard's game-winning 1-yard
touchdown catch from Eli Manning

December 24, 2011
vs. Jets

Victor Cruz's 99-yard
touchdown from Eli Manning

Ahmad Bradshaw's
14-yard touchdown run

January 1, 2012
vs. Dallas

Victor Cruz's 74-yard touchdown
from Eli Manning

January 8, 2012
vs. Atlanta

Eli Manning's 72-yard
touchdown to Hakeem Nicks

February 5, 2012
Super Bowl XLVI

Lawrence Tynes' game-winning
field goal

Victor Cruz's 2-yard touchdown
from Eli Manning

Mario Manningham's 38-yard catch
from Eli Manning

Ahmad Bradshaw's
game-winning touchdown

# 6

## NFC Wild Card Playoff
## vs. ATLANTA

January 8, 2012 · MetLife Stadium · Giants 24 – Falcons 2

Using a smothering defense and an opportunistic, big-play offense, the Giants routed the Atlanta Falcons, 24-2, in their NFC Wild Card Game. It was the Giants first postseason victory since Super Bowl XLII and their first home playoff win since the 2000 NFC Championship Game triumph over the Minnesota Vikings.

The game began poorly for the Giants offense. They punted on each of their first three possessions, and on their fourth series Eli Manning threw the ball away while being tackled in the end zone by Falcons safety James Sanders. The officials ruled that no receiver was in the vicinity and penalized Manning for intentional grounding, resulting in a safety and two points for Atlanta.

Those would be the only points the Falcons scored, as the Giants defense was dominant. Atlanta managed just 64 yards on the ground, including 41 on 15 carries by running back Michael Turner, who ran for 1,340 yards during the regular season. The Giants stopped the Falcons on 10 of 14 third-down attempts and on all three of their fourth-down conversion tries, including a pair of fourth-and-one quarterback sneaks by Matt Ryan.

Manning fared much better, completing 23 of 32 passes for a total of 277 yards and setting a career postseason high with three touchdown passes: 4 yards and 72 yards to Hakeem Nicks and 27 yards to Mario Manningham. The Giants also scored on a 22-yard field goal by Lawrence Tynes. Brandon Jacobs ran for a career postseason-high 92 yards, and Ahmad Bradshaw added 63 as the Giants ran for 172 yards, 50 more than their previous high in 2011.

"It was great to have a home playoff game and to have our fans involved as much as they were. We played outstanding defense and that set the tone for everything else that happened in the game. It was wonderful to see." —Tom Coughlin

*Above top*: Chase Blackburn, Linval Joseph and Rocky Bernard get together during the first half of a 24-2 NFC Wild Card home win over Atlanta. *Above bottom*: Steve Weatherford puts it down and Lawrence Tynes kicks it through. *Opposite*: Mario Manningham slips past Atlanta's James Sanders and Dunta Robinson for a 27-yard touchdown.

Hakeem Nicks leaps to catch a 4-yard touchdown pass over the Falcons Dominique Franks to put the Giants ahead.

Justin Tuck just barely misses Matt Bosher's punt.

*Above left*: Jerrel Jernigan returns a kick 27 yards. *Above right*: Brandon Jacobs breaks away from Atlanta's William Moore in the first half.

Eli Manning delivers the ball to Ahmad Bradshaw for one of his 14 carries.

Victor Cruz and Justin Tuck enjoy the Giants' victory.

*Above left*: Tyler Sash wraps up the Falcons star TE Tony Gonzalez. *Above right*: Hakeem Nicks poses alongside Jake Ballard after scoring a touchdown.

# TRUE GIANTS
## MICHAEL BOLEY
Linebacker

Because of injuries, the Giants defense changed week to week. With all the spot duty, Michael Boley emerged as the glue that held it all together, becoming the play-caller on defense. His consistency and veteran leadership helped the team usher in a rookie class that included defensive players whose contributions were needed immediately. Soft-spoken off the field, he is anything but that when he's on it and finished second on the team in tackles with 91. It wasn't coincidence that Boley's two-game absence due to injury came in the middle of the Giants' four-game losing skid. When he returned to the lineup, the defense improved markedly and never allowed more than 20 points in the postseason—none in the first round of the playoffs against the Falcons, who scored only on a safety. Boley had 27 tackles in the playoffs, including 10 in Super Bowl XLVI against Tom Brady and the Patriots.

Repeating a feat they accomplished four years earlier, the Giants traveled to Wisconsin in January and stunned the top-seeded Packers in the playoffs. Undaunted by Green Bay's league-best 15-1 regular season record, the Giants delivered another terrific defensive effort and Eli Manning fired three touchdown passes en route to defeating the defending Super Bowl Champion Packers, 37-20, in their NFC Divisional Playoff Game.

Packers quarterback Aaron Rodgers threw two touchdown passes and kicker Mason Crosby added a pair of field goals, but the Giants defense played superbly, holding a Green Bay team that had averaged 40.1 points at home to half that, registering four sacks—two each by defensive end Osi Umenyiora and linebacker Michael Boley—recovering three fumbles, and clinching the game with a timely interception of Rodgers by safety Deon Grant. Fellow safety Antrel Rolle logged eight unassisted stops on the day, and Boley led the way with nine tackles, eight of them solo.

For his part, Manning completed 21 of 33 passes for a career playoff record 330 yards and three touchdowns: 4 yards to Mario Manningham, 37 yards to Hakeem Nicks and a 66-yard Hail Mary to Nicks on the final play before halftime. Brandon Jacobs found the end zone on a 14-yard run, and Lawrence Tynes made sure the final score was not close with field goals of 31, 23 and 35 yards.

"This team knows how to win on the road. Right now, it just seems like it's our time." —Justin Tuck

*Clockwise from top left*: Deon Grant tackles Packers QB Aaron Rodgers during a 37-20 road win in the NFC Divisional Playoff Game; Aaron Ross buries the Packers Jordy Nelson; Brandon Jacobs plows ahead on one of his nine carries. *Opposite*: Eli Manning completed 21 of 33 pass attempts for 330 yards and three touchdowns.

Hakeem Nicks comes down with a Hail Mary touchdown in front of the Packers Charles Woodson at the end of the first half.

*Above left*: Ahmad Bradshaw breaks free from Green Bay's A.J. Hawk. *Above right*: D.J. Ware tangles with the Packers Ryan Pickett.

Antrel Rolle breaks up a pass intended for Green Bay's Greg Jennings.

Packers QB Aaron Rodgers gets a hug from Michael Boley and a shove from Corey Webster.

*Above left*: Victor Cruz makes yet another big catch in his breakout season. *Above right*: The Packers Desmond Bishop can't catch Travis Beckum.

Jake Ballard jukes Green Bay's Charlie Peprah, *left*, and Morgan Burnett on this 17-yard reception.

# TRUE GIANTS
## HAKEEM NICKS
Wide Receiver

The Giants' wide receivers confirmed in the playoffs what they had demonstrated throughout the regular season— they are one of the NFL's most talented groups. In his third NFL season, Nicks put together his second consecutive 1,000-yard season while he and Victor Cruz became the first Giants tandem to each record 1,000 yards in the same year. Nicks had a career-best 1,192 yards and seven touchdowns in the regular season on 76 catches. However, he was just getting started. In the four playoff games, Nicks had more than 100 yards in three of them and showed everyone he had the breakaway speed to complement his sure hands. He scored touchdowns on receptions of 72 and 66 yards in the first two games. And in the victory in Green Bay, Nicks delivered one of the most memorable plays of the season by catching a Hail Mary from Eli Manning as time expired in the first half. The 37-yard touchdown gave the Giants a 20-10 lead going into the locker room against the then-defending Super Bowl champs. Nicks went on to lead all receivers in Super Bowl XLVI, slashing the Patriots for 109 yards on 10 receptions.

# 8 NFC Championship Game
## at SAN FRANCISCO
January 22, 2012 · Candlestick Park · Giants 20 – 49ers 17 Overtime

For the second time in five seasons, the Giants claimed the NFC crown. Battling steady rains and heavy winds, New York capped a thrilling 20-17 victory over the San Francisco 49ers at Candlestick Park when Lawrence Tynes drilled a 31-yard field goal with 7:54 elapsed in overtime.

The 49ers scored on a 25-yard field goal by kicker David Akers and touchdown passes of 73 and 28 yards from quarterback Alex Smith to tight end Vernon Davis. The Giants had numerous big-time contributors on offense, defense and special teams. Despite being sacked six times, Eli Manning set Giants postseason records with 58 pass attempts and 32 completions. He threw for 316 yards and two touchdowns, one to tight end Bear Pascoe, his first as a professional, and the other to Mario Manningham on a third-and-15 play that gave the Giants a 17-14 lead with 8:34 remaining in the fourth quarter. Victor Cruz contributed 10 receptions for 142 yards, including eight for 125 in the first half, and Ahmad Bradshaw totaled 126 yards from scrimmage, including 74 on the ground.

Linebacker Chase Blackburn, unemployed until the week after Thanksgiving, had a team-high seven tackles (five solo), and Jason Pierre-Paul added six tackles (five solo), a half-sack and he deflected a pass. Punter Steve Weatherford recorded a 40.6-yard net average on a franchise postseason record 12 punts—the last of which set up the game-winning field goal when 49ers punt returner Kyle Williams got stripped by Jacquian Williams and teammate Devin Thomas recovered the fumble.

Five plays later, Tynes split the uprights, setting up a Super Bowl rematch for the ages.

66 It's my second NFC Championship game and my second game-winner. It's amazing, I had a dream about this; it was from 42, not 31. I was so nervous before the game. I'm usually pretty cool, but there was something about tonight. I knew I was going to have to make a kick. 99 —Lawrence Tynes

*Above*: Lawrence Tynes reacts after kicking the 31-yard game-winning field goal during the 20-17 overtime road win in the NFC Championship game against San Francisco. *Opposite*: Bear Pascoe's first-ever touchdown tied the score in the second quarter.

*Above left*: Coach Coughlin encourages his troops. *Above right*: Victor Cruz and Hakeem Nicks developed into one of the league's most dynamic receiving duos.

*Above left*: Eli Manning signals a touchdown alongside Kevin Boothe. *Above right*: Chase Blackburn drops the 49ers Anthony Dixon to the soggy turf.

Despite the nasty conditions, Eli Manning completed 32 of 58 pass attempts for 316 yards, two touchdowns with no interceptions.

Ahmad Bradshaw shoots a gap on the way to compiling 74 yards on 20 carries.

Jacquian Williams strips the ball from 49ers punt returner Kyle Williams, setting up the Giants game-winning field goal.

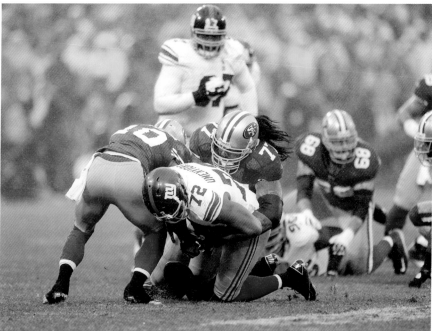
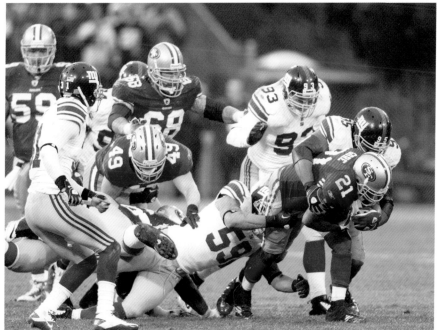

*Clockwise from top left*: Derrick Martin, Prince Amukamara and Chase Blackburn take a knee during an injury timeout; Osi Umenyiora scrambles to recover a fumble; Ahmad Bradshaw stiff arms San Francisco's Patrick Willis; 49ers Frank Gore gets gang tackled by the Big Blue defense.

*Above left*: Mario Manningham catches a touchdown pass in front of the 49ers Tramaine Brock to regain the lead. *Above right*: Jason Pierre-Paul delivered another stellar performance with six tackles.

Lawrence Tynes kicks the game-winner in overtime, earning the Giants a trip to Super Bowl XLVI.

# TRUE GIANTS
## JUSTIN TUCK
Defensive End

The defensive captain endured one of his most taxing seasons in 2011 but ultimately peaked in the postseason, becoming the dominant player the NFL is accustomed to seeing. Battling neck, groin and shoulder problems throughout the season, Tuck missed four of the first six games of the season, including the opener. After the Week 7 bye, Tuck returned against the Dolphins and assisted on a sack. But those who know Tuck could see he still wasn't himself. Despite starting the last nine games of the regular season, Tuck finished the regular season with just five sacks, his lowest total since 2006. But when the playoffs began, Tuck symbolized the team's "All In" mentality and turned it on down the stretch while battling his numerous ailments. After recording 1.5 sacks in the NFC Championship in San Francisco, Tuck had a dominant performance against New England in Super Bowl XLVI, just as he had against the Patriots in Super Bowl XLII four years earlier. He forced Patriots quarterback Tom Brady to commit intentional grounding in the end zone on New England's first offensive play, a safety that gave the Giants an early 2-0 lead. He went on to sack Brady twice in the second half, including one for a 6-yard loss on third down during the Patriots' final drive with 36 seconds remaining in the game. Had there been a runner-up to the Super Bowl MVP Award, Tuck's name would have been at the top.

# 9

## Super Bowl XLVI
## vs. NEW ENGLAND
February 5, 2012 · Lucas Oil Stadium · Giants 21 – Patriots 17

I t was a magnificent case of Déjà Blue.

No one does fourth-quarter comebacks like Eli Manning, and in the season's ultimate game he executed a true masterpiece on football's grandest stage—again. In a game that was eerily similar to Super Bowl XLII four years earlier, the key drive gained momentum with a miracle catch by a Giants wide receiver—again. The Giants scored the winning touchdown in the final minute of the game—again. And the Giants defeated the New England Patriots to become World Champions—again.

Tom Brady helped the Giants' cause in the first quarter, gifting New York two points after being flagged for intentional grounding in his own end zone that resulted in a safety. Manning connected with Victor Cruz for a 2-yard touchdown that put the Giants up 9-0, but the Patriots countered, scoring 17 unanswered points on a Steve Gostkowski 29-yard field goal and two Brady scoring strikes, to running back Danny Woodhead and tight end Aaron Hernandez. Midway through the third quarter the Patriots led 17-9.

But history would happily repeat itself for the Giants and their fans. Lawrence Tynes booted a pair of third-quarter field goals, from 38 and 33 yards, and then late in the fourth quarter Manning engineered a 9-play, 88-yard drive sparked by a perfect 38-yard throw to Mario Manningham. Ahmad Bradshaw finished things off, scoring on a 6-yard run with just 57 seconds remaining in the game.

Tom Brady could not match the last-second heroics of Manning, who completed his first nine passes and 30 of 40 overall for 296 yards and a touchdown—an effort that earned the Giants quarterback his second Pete Rozelle Trophy as the Super Bowl's Most Valuable Player. In defeating the Patriots by a final score of 21-17, the Giants won the fourth Super Bowl and eighth championship in franchise history.

The greatest feeling in professional sports
is to win the Super Bowl.   —Tom Coughlin

*Above:* Tom Coughlin hoists the franchise's fourth Vince Lombardi Trophy following the Giants thrilling 21-17 win over the Patriots in Super Bowl XLVI. *Opposite:* Giants fans were "All In" in Indianapolis.

Osi Umenyiora locks horns with the Patriots Matt Light.

Eli Manning keeps his cool as he leads the Giants' comeback.

Bear Pascoe pushes to get past the Patriots James Ihedigbo.

*Above left*: Kenny Phillips, Jacquian Williams and Deon Grant blanket Patriots TE Aaron Hernandez. *Above right*: Victor Cruz breaks into his signature salsa dance after scoring on 2-yard touchdown reception.

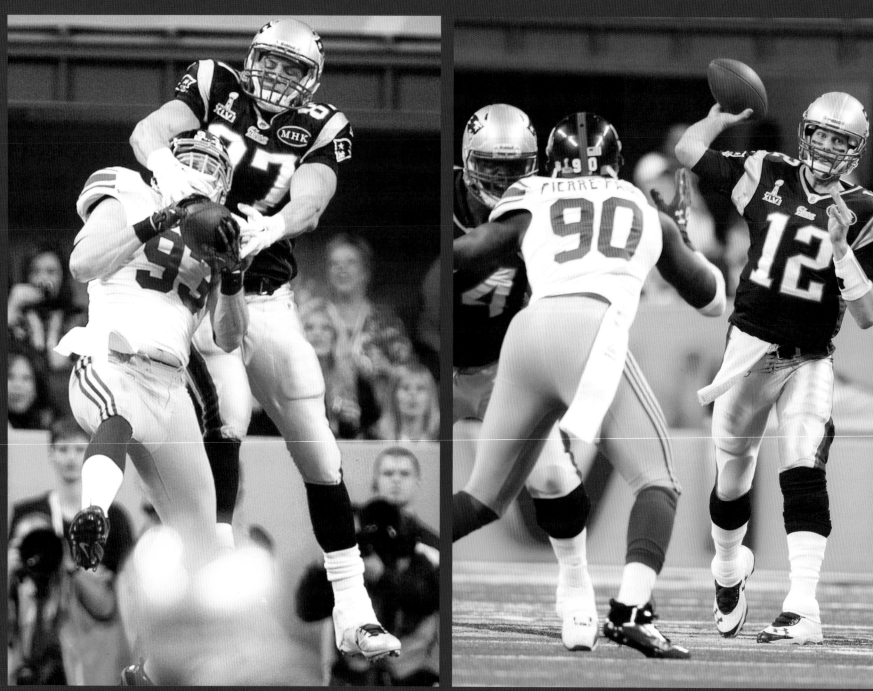

*Above left*: Chase Blackburn thwarts a Patriots drive by picking off a pass intended for the Patriots Rob Gronkowski in the fourth quarter. *Above right*: Jason Pierre-Paul keeps the pressure on Tom Brady.

Ahmad Bradshaw puts a move on New England's Kyle Arrington.

Mario Manningham snares a 38-yard pass from Manning, one of his five receptions on the day.

*Above left*: Brandon Jacobs runs just beyond the grasp of the Patriots defense. *Above right*: Hakeem Nicks makes an acrobatic catch—one of his game-high 10 receptions—over New England's Alex Molden.

*Clockwise from top left*: Henry Hynoski sprints past the horde of photographers swarming MVP Eli Manning; Osi Umenyiora rejoices with defensive coordinator Perry Fewell; confetti flies over an exhausted and emotional Antrel Rolle (with teammate Ramses Barden); this scene in Times Square was more festive than New Year's Eve.

Giants offensive and defensive captains Eli Manning and Justin Tuck revel in their accomplishment.

Special teams captain Zak DeOssie tells the world that Big Blue is back on top.

Fans young and old came out for the parade through the Canyon of Heroes; attendance estimates topped one million people.

*Clockwise from top left*: Victor Cruz feeling the love; Governor Andrew M. Cuomo, Giants matriarch Ann Mara and Eli Manning bask in the glory; New York's finest celebrate football's finest; two fans make snow angels in some of the 40 tons of confetti used in the parade.

*Clockwise from left*: Antrel Rolle and Jason Pierre-Paul flank Naughty by Nature's Vin Rock during the rally at MetLife Stadium following the parade; Hakeem Nicks signs autographs for elated fans; Ahmad Bradshaw poses with his Super Bowl XLVI ring at Tiffany & Co. on May 16, 2012; David Diehl shows off his new bling alongside his pinkie ring from Super Bowl XLII.

*Clockwise from top left*: Justin Tuck, Dave Tolleson, Linval Joseph, Rocky Bernard, Mathias Kiwanuka, Justin Trattou, defensive line coach Robert Nunn and Jason Pierre-Paul proudly display their Super Bowl XLVI rings at Tiffany & Co.

President Barack Obama receives a signed Super Bowl football and a personalized New York Giants jersey from team captains Zak DeOssie, Justin Tuck and Eli Manning.

Tom Coughlin addresses the gathering during a ceremony on the South Lawn of the White House on June 8, 2012.

# Afterword

## BY ELI MANNING

I'm not worried about my legacy. I'm worried about winning championships for the New York Giants—for my teammates, my coaches and our supporters. We've all worked hard. This is a team game. You play for your teammates and the players, the coaches and the organization that helped you get here. This isn't about bragging rights. This is a lot bigger. This is about a team, a franchise being named World Champions. That is the ultimate goal. That's the only thing that's important, finding a way to get a victory.

All last season we kept our confidence. When you lose four games in a row, that can really test a team. We played a lot of those games tough. We had talent, but we weren't playing our best at that point. We had to make a few adjustments and play a little smarter. The win at Dallas was huge win for us. To come back from being down by 12 points in the fourth quarter, to score two touchdowns and get a blocked field goal to win the game—that was an emotional win. The energy in that locker room was exciting. Everybody got that winning feeling again and said, "We have to ride this momentum." Sure enough, we were able to win a couple of big games—against the Jets and again against the Cowboys—just to get into the playoffs. Our defense was playing outstanding. Offensively, we were playing smarter, not turning the ball over, not making mistakes, being effective and running the ball better than we had at the start of the season. Everything seemed to be coming around, and we were starting to play our best football.

After beating Atlanta in the first round of the playoffs at home, we knew we were on the right path—but we also knew it was about to get a lot tougher as we had to win on the road once again. We fended off a great Green Bay team and a tough, physical San Francisco team before defeating a favored New England team in the Super Bowl. That game

Eli Manning cemented his legacy by winning his second Super Bowl in eight seasons as a Giant.

really embodied the way our whole season went; we never lost confidence, and we put together yet another fourth-quarter comeback that our fans won't soon forget.

I know that as a team and as an organization, we're out for more. We will try to become an even better team in 2012. The motivation is always trying to improve, always trying to get better. You can't worry about winning a championship next year because you know how difficult that is. You know there are a lot of things that have to happen and a lot of things you can't control, but you can control making sure you are doing everything you can to be prepared. We're making sure we do everything, both mentally and physically, to be ready as we turn the page to a new season. We are ready to defend out title. We are All In.

# Acknowledgments

### SKYBOX PRESS

*Editor:* Scott Gummer

*Publisher:* Peter Gotfredson

*Creative Director:* Nate Beale

*Project Manager:* Victoria Scavo

*Contributing Writer:* Kevin Toyama

### NEW YORK GIANTS

Mike Stevens

Don Sperling

Doug Murphy

Michael Eisen

Dan Salamone

### SPECIAL THANKS TO

Pat Hanlon, Peter John-Baptiste, Bill Heller, Debra Agosta; Matthew Morgado; Mike Shayotovich, Kevin O'Sullivan; John Sabo, Bob O'Keefe, Bill Lambe, Nick Johnson; Bill Lohr, Jason Bulger; Marti Malovany, Marty McGrath; Ken Coburn, Mike Gotfredson, Edward Burns, Frank Pellegrino and Frank Pellegrino, Jr.

### PHOTOGRAPHY

All images from AP Images except where otherwise credited: Alex Brandon, Ben Liebenberg, Bill Haber, Bill Kostroun, Charles Dharapak, Charles Krupa, Darron Cummings, David Drapkin, David Duprey, David J. Phillip, David Stluka, Elise Amendola, Eric Gay, Evan Pinkus, G. Newman Lowrance, Greg Trott, James D Smith, Jeffrey Phelps, John Minchillo, Julio Cortez, Kathy Willens, Kevin Terrell, Marcio Jose Sanchez, Mark Lennihan, Matt Ludtke, Matt Slocum, Matt York, Michael Conroy, Michael Dwyer, Michael Perez, Mike Roemer, Pat Semansky, Paul Connors, Paul Jasienski, Paul Sakuma, Paul Sancya, Paul Spinelli, Perry Knotts, Peter Morgan, Susan Walsh, Tom DiPace, Tom Hauck, Tomasso Derosa, Tony Gutierrez, Winslow Townson, Waco Tribune Herald/Jose Yau.

Library of Congress Cataloging-in-Publication Data available.

ISBN: 978-1-4197-0724-7

Manufactured in China

10 9 8 7 6 5 4 3 2 1

Published by Skybox Press, an imprint of Luxury Custom Publishing, LLC.
Distributed in North America by Abrams, an imprint of ABRAMS.

3920 Conde Street
San Diego, CA 92110
www.skyboxpress.com

115 West 18th Street
New York, NY 10011
www.abramsbooks.com